GROWING UP IN THE SIXTIES

Rebecca Hunter

HODDER
Wayland

Produced for Hodder Wayland by
Discovery Books Ltd
Unit 3, 37 Watling Street, Leintwardine, Shropshire SY7 0LW, England

First published in 2001 by Hodder Wayland, an imprint of Hodder Children's Books

© Copyright 2001 Hodder Wayland

British Library Cataloguing in Publication Data

Hunter, Rebecca,
    Growing up in the sixties
    1. Children - Great Britain - Social life and customs -
Juvenile literature 2. Great Britain - Social conditions-
20th century - Juvenile literature 3. Great Britain - Social
life and customs - 1945 - - Juvenile literature
    I. Title
    941 ' . 0856 ' 0922

    ISBN 0 7502 3547 0

Printed and bound in Grafiasa, Porto, Portugal.

Designer: Ian Winton
Editor: Rebecca Hunter

Hodder Children's Books would like to thank the following for the loan of their material:

Hulton Getty: Cover, (left), page 8 (both), 9, 10 (bottom) Caroline Gillies, 11 (top), 15 (top), 17, 20 (top), 21 Tim Graham, 22 (top), 23 (bottom) Burkett, 24 (top), 26 (top), 29 (top) Paul Fierez, 29 (bottom), 30 (both); **Jim Tonkin:** page 17; **The Robert Opie Picture Collection:** page 16 (bottom), 22 (bottom), 23 (top), 25 (bottom); **Topham Picture Point:** Cover, (right).

Hodder Children's Books
A division of Hodder Headline Limited
338 Euston Road
London NW1 3BH

CONTENTS

THE 1960s

For many people the 1960s was a decade of fun. It was a time for young people and the chance to be different. Britain led the world in fashion, design and pop music. Everyone had new ideas of how things should look. In this book, four people tell us what it was like to grow up in the sixties.

MEENA BEDI

Meena Bedi was born in 1957 in India. In 1959 her family emigrated to Northern Ireland and she grew up in a small town called Cookstown.

▶ Meena in 1960 aged 3.

PETER BRIDGE

Peter Bridge was born in 1956 in Shropshire. He still lives and works on the farm he grew up on.

▶ Peter in 1961 aged 5.

GILL HUMPHREY

Gill Humphrey was born in 1956 and lived with her parents and brother in a London suburb.

▶ Gill in 1961 aged 5.

NIGEL DUMBELL

Nigel Dumbell was born in 1953 in Southend. He has one older sister and the family lived in Thorpe Bay, Essex.

▶ Nigel in 1962 aged 9.

THE SWINGING SIXTIES

People often call the sixties the 'swinging sixties'. After the hard years of the 40s and 50s, it was a much happier decade with new fashions, designs and new music. The country was prosperous and many families had more money to spend and more leisure time than ever before.

Gill

In the 1960s we lived in an old, Victorian house in the London suburb of Leytonstone. It was a large house with several floors and a cellar. We lived in the downstairs rooms, and Mr and Mrs Spratt lived upstairs. They were very kind to my brother and me, leaving chocolate out for us in the hall and taking us out on shopping trips at weekends.

For most of the sixties, there was plenty of work available. In some areas there were not enough people to do the work and people were recruited from abroad. Many Commonwealth immigrants settled in London, the Midlands and other parts of the UK. They brought with them new sorts of food, clothes, music and religion.

Meena

My family moved to Northern Ireland from India in 1959 when I was two years old. My father had been offered a grant to set up a business, in order to generate employment for the local people. The early years were very difficult as my father worked very hard and my mother was very homesick for India. She spoke very little English and knew few people. She often cried all day and I had to comfort her.

HOUSING

In the 1960s many people were well-off enough to buy their first homes. Others however, remained in poverty. In 1965 there were more than 3 million people living in slum housing. The government and local councils built many new homes in the sixties.

In many cities, high-rise flats were built as a quick and cheap solution to the housing problem. Many people thought they were ugly and they created problems for the people living in them. They were dangerous for young children and there was nowhere for them to play.

Sixties architecture will also be remembered for some dramatic building designs. Materials such as concrete and glass were used to build some striking new buildings.

SHOPPING

Several things happened to change the experience of shopping in the sixties. Most households had a fridge, if not a freezer, and so people did not need to shop every day. Shops began to change too. Supermarkets opened up all over the country.

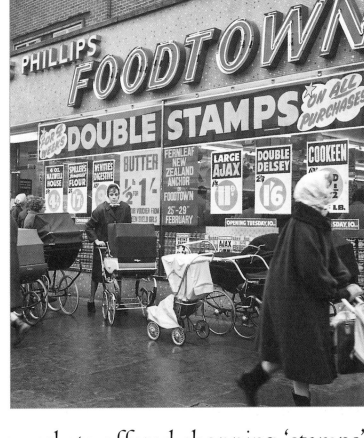

Most people enjoyed the experience of self-service shopping and the wide range of goods available. Many supermarkets offered shopping 'stamps' as an incentive to buy. The stamps were given out as you bought things and when you had enough, you could exchange them for gifts chosen from a catalogue.

Gill

In 1968, my family moved out of London to a village in Sussex. There were lots of big, new housing estates and a shopping centre with a supermarket. It was very small, but it was a new experience for us shopping with a trolley.

WORKING LIFE

The sixties was a good time to be in business. There were grants available for people to start new ventures and the public had money to spend on consumer goods and fashions.

Meena

My father opened a clothes store called the Fashion House. It was a large shop on two floors and sold ladies' and children's fashions. He employed between six and seven sales women. This picture shows me at the opening of the Fashion House. My cousin and I had to present a bouquet of flowers to a television celebrity.

EQUAL OPPORTUNITIES

In the sixties, more and more women were choosing to go out to work rather than stay at home. However, they were paid far less than men. In 1967 a man working in a factory was paid about £21 a week, but a woman was paid only £10 a week for doing the same work. It wasn't until the Equal Pay Act was passed in 1970 that women had to be paid the same as men.

FARMING

Farming in the sixties was very different to how it is today. There were many more farms, and the size of each was smaller. Farms were less mechanized than they are now and so they needed more men to work on them.

FOOT AND MOUTH DISEASE

Probably the biggest problem of the decade for farmers, was the outbreak of foot and mouth disease. In October 1967, the first case was found in Shropshire and within weeks it had become the worst outbreak British farmers had ever encountered. In eight months, animals on 2,364 farms got the disease and nearly 430,000 were slaughtered.

Peter

On Saturday 16 December the Ministry of Agriculture vets confirmed that one of our calves had foot and mouth disease. By Monday it was all over. We had to slaughter **200** cattle, **118** sheep and over **400** pigs. Diggers and excavators arrived and dug huge holes to bury the bodies.

Peter's pony was the only animal on the farm to survive the foot and mouth epidemic.

School in the Sixties

Primary School

At the age of five, children went to infant school which was followed at seven by junior or primary schools. Many new schools were built in the sixties to accommodate the children of the post-war baby boom. These schools were a big improvement on the old, cramped schools. They were often built at the edge of towns where there was room for spacious buildings and outdoor activities.

Gill

When I was seven I moved up to the junior school. Here we were streamed according to ability. The **A** stream was for clever children, **B** was for average and **C** was for slow children. I was in the **B** class but I envied the **C** children as they had the nicest teacher. We got gold or silver stars as a reward for good work and we had to write **100** lines as a punishment. The cane was still used in schools at this time, but I don't remember anyone ever getting it.

Peter

My sister and I went to a very small primary school. There were only two teachers and about **30** children. Each Christmas we put on a play. In **1963** it was Aladdin. That year the winter was extremely severe.

The week of the play we had a huge fall of snow. It was **3m (10ft)** deep in some drifts. We had to struggle to school on foot because we didn't want to miss the play.

For many children, sport was the most popular activity on the curriculum. Many of the new schools had playing fields for the first time and could expand the number of sports they offered.

Nigel

My friends were all keen supporters of Southend Football Club and we went to see them play whenever they were at home. I also saw them play in the **FA Cup** against Chelsea. We all wanted to be footballers when we grew up. None of us succeeded. This picture shows me in my junior school football team.

COMPREHENSIVES

Until the 1960s, most children had to sit an exam called the 11 Plus in their last year at primary school. If they passed this they went to a grammar school or technical school, and if they didn't they went to a secondary modern. Grammar and technical schools offered children the chance to do exams and go on to university. In secondary modern schools the emphasis was on practical subjects.

Many people thought this system was unfair and that children should not be tested and selected at this young age. As a result, the government introduced a single type of secondary school, the comprehensive. Comprehensives would ensure that all children went to the same school and had the same opportunities.

Sports Day at Wigmore Comprehensive School, built in 1963.

Gill

When I was 11 I was sent to Sidney Burnell Comprehensive School. It was one of the first comprehensive schools in East London and was very forward-looking. The teachers were all young and enthusiastic and the children all got on well together. I thought it was a wonderful school and was very happy there.

Teaching methods began to change as teachers encouraged children to find out information for themselves rather than copy it off the blackboard. Record players, tape recorders and television sets began to appear in the classrooms and field trips and project work became popular.

Peter

One year my school did a field trip to the Cairngorms. We were supposed to be learning about climbing and surviving in the snow. We camped for a week near Loch Avon. One night there was a huge storm which blew away half our tents. Our teacher decided to abandon the camp, and we had to walk through the night - and the snow and wind - back to the base camp.

HAVING FUN

Sixties children had no electronic games or computers to entertain them. They often made their own toys and invented their own games.

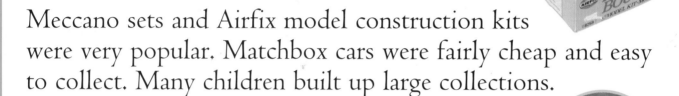

Meccano sets and Airfix model construction kits were very popular. Matchbox cars were fairly cheap and easy to collect. Many children built up large collections.

Nigel

I had a large Airfix model collection.
Most of my models were aeroplanes - they were the easiest to make.
I once tried making the Lord Mayor's coach which was very difficult. In this picture, my friend Andy and I are making the Queen Mary ocean liner.

RADIO

The invention of small, cheap transistor radios with batteries meant that many young people could buy their own radio. Many unauthorized 'pirate' radio stations started up that played mainly pop music. Radio Caroline operated from a boat in the English Channel and was very popular with teenagers.

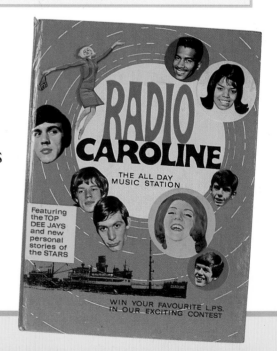

TELEVISION

Television had started up slowly after the war. By the end of the sixties more than 9 out of 10 households had one. By the mid-sixties there were several programmes available for children. In 1967 colour television broadcasts began.

1968: Blue Peter presenters show off the puppies belonging to their guide dog for the blind.

Gill

When I was very young, my favourite programmes were the Woodentops and Bill and Ben. Later I enjoyed cartoons like Yogi Bear and Huckleberry Hound. One programme that my brother and I watched, although it scared us terribly, was Doctor Who, which started in 1963. We watched most of it from behind the sofa!

THEN & NOW

• In the 60s, all programmes finished at 11.00pm. Now television can be watched 24 hours a day.

CLASSES AND CLUBS

Parents in the sixties had more money to spend on their children. They wanted their children to have the chance to do things they had missed out on when they were growing up in the difficult years of the 30s and 40s.

GIRL GUIDES AND BOY SCOUTS

Many children enjoyed belonging to girl guide or boy scout groups. This gave them the chance to take part in hobbies and activities, meet new friends and to go on holiday trips.

Nigel

Between the ages of **8** and **10**, I went to cub scouts every Thursday afternoon after school. The main reason I went was for **Cub Camp** in the summer holidays. We were only camping locally, in a field, but it was fun to sleep under canvas and cook sausages and beans over a camp fire. I don't think we ever tried to cook anything else!

DANCING

Girls often spent Saturday mornings at dancing classes.

Gill

From the age of 4 until I was 12, all I wanted to do was dance, and be a ballerina when I grew up. My ballet school put on a concert once a year. This was the highlight of my year - better even than Christmas! One year my mother made me a frothy pink tu-tu. It was my pride and joy and I wore it whenever I could.

PONY CLUB

Children who lived in the country often belonged to the Pony Club.

Peter

For ten years I was a member of the Pony Club. In summer we had a week of Pony Club Camp at Bangor and Dee Racecourse. We spent all day grooming, mucking out and riding our ponies, and spent the nights sleeping in the stables. My best pony was called Bear and I won many rosettes and certificates on him. One year I won a silver cup for Best Stable Management. I was very proud of it.

FASHION AND MUSIC

By 1964 the United Kingdom had become the centre of young fashion. Boutiques sprang up everywhere and Carnaby Street and the King's Road in London became the trendy places to be seen.

Meena

When I was a teenager I worked in my dad's shop every Saturday. Because I was interested in fashion I had my own fashion column in the local paper. I wrote about the latest fashion trends and designed advertisements for the Fashion House. My father would often organize fashion shows presenting the latest fashions. This picture was taken in 1968 at a fashion show.

Sixties fashions used new materials and bold colours and designs. Mary Quant, a famous sixties designer, did more to change fashion than anybody else. One of her inventions was tights, for wearing with the mini skirt - the new fashion craze.

Bell-bottom jeans, skinny rib jumpers, knee-high boots and platform shoes were other new fashion trends. Trousers also became acceptable for women to wear.

Gill

Everyone at school wanted to wear their skirts short, like the fashion models. Our mums didn't approve, so we had to wait until we were out of sight of home to roll the waistbands of our skirts over until the skirt was short enough. When we came home in the afternoon, we had to make sure we remembered to roll them down again!

POP MUSIC

The 60s was the decade of pop music. The biggest influence was the Beatles who arrived on the pop scene in 1962. They had 21 UK top ten hit singles in the sixties, and in April 1964, they held the first five places in the US pop charts. In 1965 the Beatles were given the MBE by the Queen because of the number of records they had sold.

The Beatles became so popular in America and the UK that the term 'Beatlemania' was coined. Everywhere they went there were thousands of fans waiting to get a glimpse of them. Screaming fans blocked airports and caused traffic jams both sides of the Atlantic.

Nigel

Once we had a fancy dress competition at school at the end of term party. Three of my friends and I went as the Beatles. We dressed up like them and made cardboard guitars and drums out of biscuit tins. I was Paul McCartney and combed my hair forward like his.

THEN & NOW

- In 1965 a single cost 6s 8d (33p). Now a single CD costs £2.99.

Other British faces that were popular in the sixties were Cilla Black, Lulu and Cliff Richard, all of whom are still performing today.

Another big new band of the sixties was the Rolling Stones. They were very different to other groups. Their dress and approach to music was quite shocking. They were very popular with rebellious teenagers - to the horror of their parents. They became known as the best live band in the world, and their fans caused such chaos that sometimes their concerts had to be cancelled.

▲ Cliff Richard has made the most appearances on Top of the Pops, with over 80.

The Rolling Stones in concert.

TRAVELLING

The sixties saw two major changes in how people got around: they used the railways less and the roads more.

TRAINS

In 1963, a government enquiry into British Railways led to the closing of about 5,000 miles (8,000 km) of railway lines and 3,000 stations. This closure was organized by Dr Beeching and known as the 'Beeching Axe'. Nearly all small villages and many larger towns lost their railway station.

British Railways changed its name to British Rail, and introduced new carriages without separate compartments.

CARS

Many families bought their first car in the 60s.

Gill

My father had bought his first car in 1959. It was a grey Austin van that he used for work. By 1961 we had our first proper car, an Austin A40. This meant the whole family could now go out on trips. We often went on picnics at weekends.

By the end of the decade there were nearly 15 million cars in Britain. Almost half of all families had a car, and some had two.

The increase in car driving caused many problems in towns. Parking became difficult and town councils built the first multi-storey car parks to provide enough space. Yellow lines and parking meters became a familiar sight in the streets.

Meena

By the mid-sixties my family had two cars. My father drove a Ford Zephyr and my mother a Mini. This photo shows my little sister sitting on the roof of our Mini on the beach. You can see several other sixties cars in the picture.

THEN & NOW

- In the mid-60s there were 8,000 deaths a year on the road.

- This figure is now only 3,500. This has been due to speed limits, which were introduced in 1965 and the compulsory wearing of seat belts, which became law in 1983.

More Mini-magic!

MORRIS MINI-MINORS
NOW WITH HYDROLASTIC® SUSPENSION

The first Mini was produced in 1959 and over the next six years, one million cars were made.

HOLIDAYS

Although package holidays abroad had started in the fifties, most people in the sixties still holidayed in Great Britain. The increase in the number of private car owners meant that more people used their cars to go on holiday.

- In 1960, 90 per cent of holidays were taken in Great Britain. In 2000, only 52 per cent were.

Meena

We didn't go away on holiday, but we did go out on family trips every Sunday. In the summer, my family and other relatives would often drive over to Lough Neagh. We would take a picnic and spend the day enjoying the countryside and rowing on the lake.

Gill

During the war, my mother was evacuated to a village in South Wales called Ferryside. She was so happy there that this was where we always spent our holidays. It had a beautiful beach with wonderful rocks for climbing on. We enjoyed making sandcastles on the beach or paddling in the sea, but it was too dangerous to swim.

CARAVANS

People began to look for more adventurous things to do on holiday. The new family caravans were a different and fairly cheap way to take a holiday. Caravan sites became a familiar sight in the countryside and at seaside resorts.

HOLIDAY CAMPS

Holiday camps became ever more popular. They offered entertainment-packed holidays that were an enormous success with children.

Nigel

We used to go to Leysdowne Holiday Camp on the Isle of Sheppey. We stayed in little chalets and had fun doing all the activities.

There was a playground, a boating pool and a golf putting course which I liked best. There were competitions for kite making and flying, and fancy dress, but I never won any!

LIVING IN THE SIXTIES

RACE RELATIONS

In the late fifties and early sixties, thousands of immigrants came to Britain. 136,000 arrived in 1961 alone. In some areas of the country, the immigrants were well received.

Meena

The Indian community in Northern Ireland in the sixties was small but very industrious. We were held in high regard by all the local people and I was never made to feel like an outsider.

In many other parts of the country there was a great deal of racisim. The immigrants were often paid lower wages than white people would be. A lot of resentment occurred between the immigrants and the locals. The 1968 Race Relations Act made it illegal to discriminate against anyone on the grounds of race or colour.

Gill

A black family came to live next door to us. They had a daughter called Elvira who I would talk to over the fence and occasionally play with in the street. But our friendship was not encouraged. That still makes me feel sad today, and I sometimes wonder what Elvira is doing now.

THALIDOMIDE

There were many remarkable advances in medicine during the sixties, but often the disasters are better remembered. One such event was when pregnant mothers were given the drug Thalidomide. This resulted in over 400 babies being born with deformed or missing limbs. The public were horrified that a drug could be given to people without proper testing.

THE ABERFAN DISASTER

For over 50 years, the little mining village of Aberfan in Wales had been overshadowed by a huge tip of coal waste from the surrounding mines. On 21 October 1966 after heavy rains, the tip collapsed and slid down the mountainside onto the village of Aberfan. Several houses and the junior school were engulfed. Five teachers and 116 school children were killed. The miners left their work and the whole village came to help with the digging. The rescue operation took over a week and a total of 144 people lost their lives.

WORLD CUP WIN

For many people the high point of the sixties was when England beat Germany in the 1966 World Cup at Wembley. Everybody remembers where they were when the match was won.

Nigel

All my friends gathered at Andy's house to watch the World Cup. It was the most exciting match I had ever seen. Geoff Hurst scored a goal in the final few seconds of the game. The whole country seemed to celebrate for days.

MOON LANDING

On 21 July 1969 the American spacecraft *Apollo 11* landed on the Moon. The event was watched by hundreds of millions of people on their television sets. As Neil Armstrong became the first man to set foot on the Moon, he said the famous words: 'That's one small step for a man, one giant leap for mankind.'

The landing of a man on the Moon was not only the most exciting event of the decade but probably our greatest achievement of the century.

FURTHER READING

A Look at Life in - *The Sixties*   Hodder Wayland

History From Objects - *At School, In the Street, Keeping Clean* and *Toys*   Hodder Wayland

History From Photographs - *Clothes and Uniforms, Houses and Homes, Journeys, People Who Help Us, School, In the Home* and *In the Street*   Hodder Wayland

Take Ten Years - *1960s, Ken Hills* Evans Brothers

When I Was Young - *The Sixties*, Neil Thomson Franklin Watts

The 1960s, Tim Healey Franklin Watts

The A-Z of the 1960s, Ann and Ian Morrison, Breedon Books

GLOSSARY

baby boom: A time when a large number of babies were born.

boutique: A small, trendy shop that sells clothes.

consumer goods: Items bought by the public.

curriculum: An approved course of study.

discriminate: Make a distinction on the grounds of sex, race or colour.

epidemic: A widespread outbreak of a disease.

foot and mouth disease: A highly-infectious disease that affects farm animals, particularly cows, sheep and pigs.

immigration: People coming from abroad to live in Great Britain.

Ministry of Agriculture: A government department that deals with farming.

package holiday: A holiday that includes transport and accommodation.

racism: A belief that some races are better than others.

shopping stamps: Stamps that were given out by supermarkets. Stamps were collected and exchanged for gifts.

singles: Small, vinyl records were called singles because they had just one song on each side.

slum housing: Very poor or run-down housing.

INDEX